STAND AGAINST

T0047155

PREJUDICE

Izzi Howell

PowerKiDS press™

New York

Published in 2023 by The Rosen Publishing Group, Inc.
29 East 21st Street, New York, NY 10010

Editor: Izzi Howell

Designer and illustrator: Mimi Butler

Cataloging-in-Publication Data

Names: Howell, Izzi.
Title: Prejudice / Izzi Howell.
Description: New York : PowerKids Press, 2023. | Series: Stand against | Includes glossary and index.
Identifiers: ISBN 9781725339033 (pbk.) | ISBN 9781725339040 (library bound) | ISBN 9781725339057 (ebook)
Subjects: LCSH: Prejudices--Juvenile literature. | Discrimination--Juvenile literature. | Social action--Juvenile literature.
Classification: LCC HM1091.H767 2023 | DDC 303.3'85--dc23

Manufactured in the United States of America

CPSIA Compliance Information: Batch #CSPK23. For further information contact Rosen Publishing, New York, New York at 1-800-237-9932.

Find us on

CONTENTS

KNOW YOUR TARGETS: Prejudice

Prejudice is feeling a certain way about a person because of a group that they belong to, such as their religion or race. Prejudice usually refers to bad feelings, such as disliking someone or having an unfair opinion of them.

DIFFERENT GROUPS

When we think about prejudice, we often think about race, but there are many other types as well. We can be prejudiced against people who belong to certain religions or come from certain countries. People also experience prejudice because of their sexual orientation, age, gender, disability, and size. Minority groups often experience the most prejudice.

STUPID STEREOTYPES

No one likes to think that they are prejudiced. However, prejudices are sometimes hidden inside us without us realizing. They often come out in stereotypes – set ideas about everyone who belongs to a group, such as that girls aren't good at math. It's easy to think that stereotypes are silly and harmless, but they have a real impact on the way people think and behave.

BAD TO WORSE

Prejudice can lead to discrimination – unfair treatment of someone because they are part of a certain group. This can include bullying, name-calling, violence, or other serious offenses such as taking away someone's human rights. It's important to fight against prejudice of any kind to stop it from reaching this extreme stage.

THINK AND ACT

When was the last time you heard a stereotype? What could you say to someone who is stereotyping people?

 Read on for more information about different types of prejudice and how to stand against it!

MEASURE YOUR PREJUDICES

Everyone has prejudices, although most people don't realize it! Test your prejudices with this simple experiment.

You'll need: around 20 photos of people, a pen, and a notepad.

STEP 1

Put together a selection of around 20 photos of people. Print pictures off the internet or cut them out of magazines. Include a diverse mix, with people of different races, religions, genders, ages, and disabilities.

STEP 2

Lay out the pictures on a table. Look at the pictures and ask yourself the following questions about the people in the photos.

Who do you think ...

... has been to college?

... is a politician?

... is a stay-at-home parent?

... has been arrested?

... is unemployed?

... you would ask for directions in the street?

... is a famous actor?

... likes to play football?

You can choose one person or a few people for each question. Write down your answers so that you don't forget them.

STEP 3

Look back at your answers and think about why you chose them. Can you see any patterns? Think about common prejudices that may have affected your judgement of these people. Challenge yourself to think beyond these stereotypes more often to see if you can be more open-minded.

Did you choose a woman for the stay-at-home parent question? In our society, the prejudice that women are better at looking after children than men is very widespread. Most people will automatically choose women for this answer, even if they don't agree that only women should be responsible for childcare.

STEP 4

Ask a friend or a member of your family to repeat the experiment with the same set of photos. Compare your answers – did you answer in the same way?

WHERE DOES PREJUDICE COME FROM?

Prejudice comes from many different places — it's hard to pinpoint just one. Everything around us affects the way in which we see the world, and that includes how we think about other people.

PARENT TO CHILD

Our families are one of our biggest influences. Just as they help us to grow and learn, they can also influence us in negative ways, such as passing on prejudices. What we as children hear our parents saying has a huge impact on what we grow up thinking to be true — and we don't usually question if it's right or wrong.

PEER PRESSURE

Our friends also influence what we think. If all our friends think something is true, it's easier to agree with them and go along with peer pressure, rather than be the odd one out. This can lead to a situation where we find ourselves repeating information that we don't actually think is true.

STEREOTYPES ON SCREEN

The media and entertainment that we enjoy can also pass on prejudices. TV shows, films, books, and even songs often include stereotypical characters or situations. At first, these characters can seem funny, but over time, it's easy to start believing that the stereotype can be applied to all people of that character's race, religion, or sexual orientation, for example.

FAKE NEWS

Nowadays, the internet and fake news stories are powerful tools in spreading prejudice. Fake news is false information that is designed to trick people into believing that it is true. It often plays on common prejudices, such as the dangers of certain groups. People can easily share fake news stories on social media without any restrictions. Some websites, and even newspapers, also publish fake news stories and incorrect, prejudiced information.

THINK AND ACT

Fake news stories and other online content are designed to stir up hatred and make people feel as if their prejudices are valid. It's important to think clearly about anything that you read on social media or on websites, and check if it is true. You can also **report prejudiced and hateful comments** on social media, so that the site can delete them.

MEASURE THE MEDIA

Try this experiment to look more closely at the characters in the films, TV shows, and books you enjoy. You might be surprised by the results!

 STEP 1 Choose a film, book, or TV episode that you like.

 STEP 2 While you watch or read, focus on the characters. See if you can check off the following rules.

Are there two female characters? ✔

Do they speak to each other? ✗

Is the conversation about anything other than a man? ✗

 STEP 3 If you can't check off all or some of them, think about what that means. Do you think it's right? Would the story change if it followed the rules above? If so, how would it change?

Women make up over half of the world's population, so statistically they should appear in most scenarios. If they don't appear, or don't get the chance to speak, it makes them seem less important than men. Seeing women portrayed in this way slowly influences us and can lead to prejudice.

STEP 4

Repeat the test, focusing on a different group of people. Are there characters of different races or religions? Are there people with disabilities or different body types? Do these people get a chance to speak? And do they get to talk about anything beyond this aspect of who they are?

Most films, books, and TV shows do not represent a diverse range of characters. Having characters from different backgrounds and with different bodies is important, as it shows that everyone's story deserves to be told. Seeing diversity in media also helps people to look beyond people's appearances and understand that everyone is equally complex, as we all have personalities, hopes, and fears.

DISCRIMINATION

People may not realize that their prejudices actually affect their behavior, and can lead them to discriminate against others. It isn't illegal to be prejudiced, but is against the law to discriminate against someone because of those prejudices.

LIMITING POTENTIAL

The effects of discrimination often begin at school. If adults don't support or encourage all students to push themselves, they may not fulfill their full potential. This limits their options in the future, such as going to college or working in their dream career. Often, adults may not even be aware that they are treating students from certain groups differently.

THINK ABOUT IT

Unfair punishment at school is also a form of discrimination. Minority groups are often more likely to be excluded than white pupils. Do you think your school gives out punishments fairly?

FIGHTING CHALLENGES

As adults, discrimination means that some people are less likely to be selected for jobs. They may also be treated badly, or even lose their jobs, because of the prejudice of their colleagues and employers. It can also be harder for some people to find homes to rent or buy, as prejudiced people can obstruct their choices in the process.

ACCIDENT OR ON PURPOSE?

Sometimes, people don't realize that they are discriminating against others. It's important to examine our prejudices so that we don't accidentally discriminate without realizing. Other times, people are aware of their prejudices but they discriminate anyway, as they think that certain people don't deserve to be treated well.

HATE CRIMES

The most extreme form of discrimination is a hate crime – a crime committed against someone because they belong (or appear to belong) to a certain group. This can range from name-calling and graffiti to violence and even murder. It is against the law to commit a hate crime. If you or someone you know experiences or witnesses a hate crime, you should talk to an adult you trust, who can help you report it to the police.

EQUAL RIGHTS

Human rights are basic things that everyone should have or be able to do, just because they are human. Access to human rights is often affected by prejudice.

UNIVERSAL HUMAN RIGHTS

In 1948, the United Nations (UN) created the Universal Declaration of Human Rights. This is a list of 30 rights that everyone around the world should have. The list includes the following rights, plus many more:

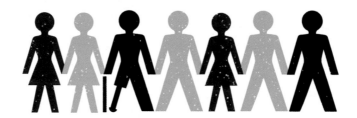

> the right to live freely and safely

> the right to be treated fairly

> the right to be able to marry and have a family

> the right to choose a job

> the right to be treated fairly at work

> the right to an education

FAIR TREATMENT

Some people are denied their basic human rights because of prejudice. They are treated unfairly because of the color of their skin, their religion, their sexual orientation, their gender, or other reasons. This goes against the basic human right that everyone should be treated fairly, whoever they are.

PREJUDICE PROBLEMS

In some countries, gay couples are not allowed to get married. This goes against the human right to be able to get married. Disabled people are often overlooked by employers and aren't treated fairly at work, which goes against their human rights to choose a job and be treated fairly at work.

THINK ABOUT IT

Research the other human rights that are included in the Universal Declaration of Human Rights. Can you think of other examples of rights that are affected by prejudice?

Many activists around the world fight every day for people's human rights and to end prejudice and discrimination. Here are some ways that you can get involved to help support these activists, raise awareness of human rights abuses, and make a change.

STEP 1

Petitions are a great way to show politicians that you want change to happen. Work with your friends to **make a petition about a human rights issue** that you care about. Get as many people as possible to sign it – you could create a fact sheet with some background information to help persuade people. When it's complete, send your petition to your government officials. If it's about an issue in another country, you could send it to that country's ambassador.

STEP 2

Research a human rights issue with a group of friends and put together a short play. It could be based on the story of a real-life activist or a fictional story based on true events. **Put on your play** at school or organize a street performance to bring your message to the wider world.

 Ask an adult about how to organize a street performance.

STEP 3

Write letters to support activists who have been discriminated against because of their work. Every year, the human rights charity Amnesty International organizes a **letter-writing campaign** to show activists that people are thinking of them. See if your class can get involved, or organize an event in your community with the help of an adult.

Find out more at:
www.amnesty.org/en/get-involved/write-for-rights/

PRIVILEGE

"Privilege" describes advantages that people have because they belong to a certain group. It can be seen as being the opposite of prejudice and discrimination (negative treatment because of the group you belong to).

TYPES OF PRIVILEGE

There are different types of privilege. Common examples include white privilege, male privilege, and straight privilege. People also experience privilege because they are rich or thin. If you have any of these privileges, it is likely that you will be treated better at school and at work, and less likely that you will experience discrimination.

ADVANTAGES

There are also specific advantages for each type of privilege. For example, thin people can find clothes in their size in any shop. Straight people are able to talk about their partners in any situation, while gay people may not feel safe to.

PRIVILEGE AND PREJUDICE

Many people are affected by both privilege and prejudice. For example, a gay man will benefit from male privilege, but may be affected by homophobia. A non-disabled, thin woman has these privileges, but may suffer because of sexism or racism, for example. We all struggle in different ways, so try to put yourself into other people's shoes and understand their situation.

STRUGGLE AND SUCCESS

It can be hard for people with privilege to understand that their lives are not like other people's. They find it hard to accept that their success might be partly connected to their privilege, rather than all the result of their own effort. It's difficult for them to understand that some people struggle to succeed because of prejudice, not because of a lack of effort.

For example, if someone's family is rich and can afford to send them to a private school with more individual attention from the teachers, their school experience will be very different from that of a student who goes to a school with crowded classes, and whose working parent doesn't have time to help them with homework. Which child do you think is more likely to get better test scores?

THINK AND ACT

People can use their privilege to help others who don't have it. They can stand up for someone if they are being bullied or use their voice to raise awareness on behalf of people who aren't being listened to. How could you use your privilege to help others?

RACE

We use the word "race" to describe groups of people who have the same shared physical characteristics, such as skin, eye, or hair colors. Prejudice and discrimination against someone because of their race is called racism.

A TERRIBLE HISTORY

In the past, white people discriminated against black people in many ways. They took black people from Africa and forced them to work as slaves in the Americas and other areas. Later, they set up segregated societies in countries such as the United States and South Africa, in which black and white people weren't allowed to use the same schools, restaurants, or other public buildings.

AN EQUAL WORLD

Despite movements toward racial equality, people are still discriminated against because of their race. Some racism is obvious and violent, such as racist hate crimes (see page 13). Other types of racial prejudice are more subtle, such as major companies only making bandages or makeup in pale skin tones.

Research shows that in the United States, black men are sent to prison for 20 percent longer than white men who commit the same crime.

BLACK LIVES MATTER

BLack Lives Matter is a famous activism movement created to protect black people's rights and draw attention to the discrimination that they face, particularly in the legal system.

The movement started in the United States when three women, **Alicia Garza**, **Patrisse Cullors**, and **Opal Tometi**, tweeted about a controversial court case using the hashtag **#BlackLivesMatter**.

Since its creation, **Black Lives Matter** has also used social media campaigns, protests, and marches to draw attention to cases where black people have been treated with excess force without any repercussions. By publicizing these stories, Black Lives Matter puts pressure on those in power to make changes and protect black people.

#blacklivesmatter

THINK AND ACT

If you are old enough to use social media, post a message about something that you think needs to change. Use a hashtag that already exists or create a new one!

BLACK HISTORY MONTH

Learn more about history and pay respect to people who are often overlooked by getting involved with Black History Month!

WHY?

In many places, white history and culture is celebrated more than that of other races. At school, students often read books by white authors and learn about famous white people. However, people of every race have actually played important roles throughout history.

Black History Month highlights these stories and helps people to learn more. It also draws attention to black experiences that can be overlooked or underrepresented, such as slavery and segregation.

HOW TO GET INVOLVED

Black History Month takes place in different months around the world, such as February in the United States and Canada and October in the United Kingdom. Here are some ideas for how you can get involved on your own, with friends and family, or with your class at school.

Read a book by a black author.

Watch a film made by a black filmmaker.

Learn poems by black poets and hold a poetry reading.

Study the artwork of a black artist.

Watch Martin Luther King Jr.'s "I Have A Dream" speech.

Find a Black History Month event in your area and go with friends or family.

Choose a black scientist or inventor and make posters celebrating their achievements. Display the posters at school.

OTHER EVENTS

Some areas focus on people of different backgrounds in other months. In the United States, May is dedicated to American and Pacific Islander heritage. LGBTQ+ Pride Month is celebrated in June every year. Why not read books or watch films made by people from these backgrounds and communities in these months, or in your own time?

CULTURAL APPROPRIATION

You may have heard the phrase "cultural appropriation" used in relation to fashion, hair, art, music, culture, or food. But what does it mean and how is it connected to prejudice and discrimination?

TAKING FROM OTHERS

Cultural appropriation is when someone takes elements of a different culture or group to which they don't belong, without acknowledging where they come from. One example is when a white person wears their hair in braided cornrows, which is a traditional black hairstyle. Cultural appropriation is usually an issue of power – someone from a majority group taking something from a minority group or culture.

NOT FAIR

It's not wrong to be inspired by other cultures. However, there are situations in which it can cause problems. It is often the case that a majority group adopts something that a minority group is discriminated against for, but then takes credit for it and benefits from it. For example, a black person might be banned from wearing braided cornrows to school or work, but the same school or office might not think to apply that restriction to a white person in braided cornrows, because this is seen more as a fashion choice rather than something cultural.

SPECIAL ITEMS

Cultural appropriation is also an issue when important cultural items are used for a different purpose that causes offense. Native American headdresses with feathers are reserved for special cultural and religious events, and can only be worn by people who have earned the right. If a non-Native American person wears one of these headdresses as a costume, it would be disrespectful.

BE RESPECTFUL

The best way to guard against cultural appropriation is with knowledge and respect. Research the backgrounds of fashion, hairstyles, and art, and learn where they come from and what they mean. If you find something that has an important cultural meaning, be respectful and leave it for that purpose.

THINK AND ACT

Think of some other ways to appreciate cultural objects without taking them for yourself. You could attend a traditional fashion show or museum exhibition, or look for a postcard of someone from the culture wearing objects that are special to them.

RELIGION

Everyone has the right to have and follow a religion. However, in many parts of the world, people are discriminated against for following certain religions.

FIGHTING FEAR

Religious prejudice often comes from ignorance, as others misunderstand what it means to follow that religion and fear it as something dangerous. The best way to fight back against this is by learning about a wide range of religions. Bringing people from different religions together also helps people with prejudices to see that we can all get along, regardless of religion.

THINK AND ACT

Look at a range of different types of news websites, such as *The Guardian*, *The New York TImes*, and *The Wall Street Journal*. How do they report on stories about religion? Do you think they are good sources of information? Why or why not?

ISLAM AND ISLAMISTS

At the moment, there is a lot of prejudice about Islam. This is partly due to the actions of a small number of fundamentalist Islamists, such as those in ISIS, who commit terrorism in the name of Islam. It's important to remember that fundamentalist Islamists do not represent the religion or Muslims as a whole. The religion of Islam encourages peace and nonviolence, so it's not fair to use these isolated incidents as an excuse for discrimination against Muslims.

RELIGIOUS PERSECUTION

In some places, people are treated terribly because of their religion. They are arrested, kept in prison, or even sentenced to death. The Holocaust – the murder of more than six million Jewish people during the Second World War – was a devastatingly extreme example of religious persecution.

RIGHT OR WRONG?

 There are some issues with aspects of religion that affect other people's human rights ...

 Followers of some religions do not believe that it is right to be gay. Should they be allowed to express their homophobic beliefs? The current situation in the United States is that anyone can disagree with homosexuality, but they can't say hateful things to gay people or discriminate against them.

 In France and some other European countries, Muslim women are not allowed to wear some head coverings in public. These countries believe that the head coverings go against the rights of women. However, banning them also goes against the rights of Muslims to wear what they want.

WHAT DO YOU THINK?

STAND AGAINST:
RELIGIOUS MISUNDERSTANDINGS

Unless you follow a religion, it can be hard to truly understand what people believe and how they worship. It's often easy to rely on stereotypes and information passed on from others who don't have all the facts. The best way to avoid misunderstandings is to learn from people in that religion, as well as your own research.

STEP 1

Which religions do people follow in your local area? How much do you know about them and what their followers believe? Organize a trip with an adult to a local religious center. Contact the leader at the center ahead of time and see if they can give you a tour and explain the different parts of the building.

STEP 2

Hold a presentation day at school. Invite people from different religions in your class to speak about their religion, what they believe, and how they worship. Allow people to ask questions to clear up any misunderstandings, making sure they are sensitive and respectful. People who are atheist or agnostic may also want to speak about why they choose not to follow a religion.

Christmas and Easter celebrations are common at some schools, but students at your school may celebrate other religious festivals. Organize an event to celebrate a religious festival. Invite all the students and teachers to get involved.

Many people who follow religions that are a minority in a country are happy to speak to others about their beliefs. However, they can sometimes feel vulnerable if they have suffered prejudice and discrimination. Don't just rely on other people to explain their religion to you. Do your own research from trustworthy sources, such as library books or encyclopedias.

>> **How would you react if you heard someone at school being prejudiced against a religion or discriminating against someone who followed that religion? Plan out what you'd do, such as discuss their prejudiced actions calmly with them, support the person being bullied, or tell a teacher.**

GENDER

Attitudes toward gender have changed a lot over the last 100 years. We are moving toward equality, but there is still a lot of sexism (prejudice and discrimination based on gender).

OLD WAYS OF THINKING

In the past, women were denied many rights. They could not vote, own property, have their own bank account, or do certain jobs. Many people considered women to be less intelligent and less capable than men. Thanks to the hard work of many activists, this is no longer the case in many places around the world.

HARMFUL STEREOTYPES

There are still many stereotypes about gender, such as that women are caring and emotional, while men are tough and strong. These stereotypes limit people's behavior – we all have emotional moments and times when we want to be tough. It hurts people to force them to behave according to gender stereotypes. Men can often experience mental health problems as a result of feeling they're not meant to express their emotions.

SCHOOL DAYS

At school, girls are often stereotyped as being better at creative subjects, while boys are considered to be better at STEM subjects (science, technology, engineering, and math). This means that many girls do not choose to study STEM subjects, which may affect their future careers.

WOMEN AT WORK

Women also struggle against prejudice in the workplace. Sexist discrimination makes it harder for them to reach the high-up leadership roles, which are still usually taken by men. Women are also paid, on average, 20–40 percent less than men for doing the same work.

 Women only hold 24 percent of the roles in national lawmaking bodies around the world.

FIGHTING FOR AN EDUCATION

In some countries, gender inequality is extreme. Many girls are still denied the right to go to school or are forced to leave school early. It isn't considered important for them to get an education, as their future will be looking after their family. Charities are working hard in these countries to improve access to schooling so that every girl can get an education.

THINK AND ACT

Hold a fundraising event at school or in your neighborhood to raise money for a charity that supports girls' education around the world. You could sell homegrown plants, secondhand books, clothes, and toys.

STAND AGAINST:
GENDER STEREOTYPES

Gender stereotypes are everywhere. These stereotypes help to spread prejudices that harm both men and women.

 YOU MAY HAVE HEARD OR EVEN SAID SOME OF THESE PHRASES:

You run/throw like a girl.
Boys don't cry. That's not ladylike.

CAN YOU THINK OF ANY MORE PHRASES TO ADD TO THE LIST?

SPREADING STEREOTYPES

These expressions reflect and spread common stereotypes about how men and women should behave. The phrases about women suggest that women are physically weak and should be calm and gentle, not strong or dominant. This is why women with strong opinions are often described as bossy, as if it's a bad thing, while strong men are described as leaders. The phrases about men suggest that they shouldn't be weak or show emotions.

Hold a campaign for your school to raise awareness of this issue.

STEP 1

Make posters to decorate your classroom and notice boards in the hallways. You could include some alternative phrases to use instead, such as "Everyone has feelings" instead of "Boys don't cry," or come up with your own slogans.

STEP 2

Ask if you can do a presentation on this topic during an assembly. You could perform a role play to show how gender stereotypes affect people, such as a boy who doesn't feel it's safe to talk about his feelings. Or include some statistics, such as that 50 percent of girls feel like they can't participate as much as they want to at school, in activities such as contributing ideas in class or leading teams.

STEP 3

Look at the after-school activities at your school, such as sports or art. Are they split along gender lines? See if a club can hold an introductory session for your class so that everyone can try it out and get involved. This will help attract a more diverse range of people to the club!

LGBTQ+

The term LGBTQ+ stands for lesbian, gay, bisexual, transgender, queer, and more. Many people with different sexual orientations and gender identities fall into this group. Over the years, the LGBTQ+ community has experienced a lot of discrimination, some of which sadly continues today.

FIGHTING FOR RIGHTS

Even in the 21st century, changing laws against homosexuality around the world has been difficult, as many people still hold prejudiced views. However, activists continue to work hard for LGBTQ+ people to have access to equal human rights globally.

Homosexuality only became legal in England in 1967. It wasn't until 2003 that it became legal across the entire United States.

EQUAL MARRIAGE

One of the most important rights for many gay couples is being recognized legally as a couple. First, gay and lesbian couples could enter into civil partnerships. Then, eventually, equal marriage was legalized in many places, giving gay people the same right to marry as straight people. However, despite this progress, many gay people still face discrimination. Bullying still often happens in schools and in some workplaces.

OTHER COUNTRIES

Around the world, 74 countries still have anti-homosexuality laws. People accused of homosexuality face punishments ranging from prison time to life imprisonment and even the death penalty. LGBTQ+ people in these countries can't live freely. They have to hide their relationships, fearing what might happen if they were exposed.

TRANS RIGHTS

Transgender people are one of the groups most likely to suffer discrimination and prejudice, which seriously affects their mental health and safety. Cisgender people (people born with the gender that they identify with) can help support trans people by using the pronouns they request, such as "she," "he," "they," or others. Listen to their needs and speak out to combat prejudice when they would like you to.

THINK AND ACT

Bathrooms can be a stressful place for people who are transgender or nonbinary (someone who does not identify with any gender). Does your school have a gender-neutral bathroom? If not, speak to your teachers and principal and see if one can be organized.

"That's so gay!" You may have heard or said this phrase before and not thought much of it. But although the expressions we use may seem harmless, they can do a lot of damage and help to spread and maintain prejudices.

The phrase "That's so gay" is often used to mean "That's so stupid" or "That's so bad." Using the word "gay" to describe something negative suggests that being gay is something negative as well. This is offensive and hurtful, and is an expression of homophobic prejudice. Some people also use homophobic insults, which adds to the idea that being gay is something to be ashamed of.

STEP 1

Don't ignore homophobic language. If you allow it to continue, it sends out the message that it's OK. Other people may even start to copy it. If you feel comfortable, say something to the person using homophobic language. Otherwise, talk to a teacher or an adult.

 In the U.S., 52 percent of LGBTQ+ young people report homophobic bullying at school.

STEP 2

Work with your classmates to come up with a list of alternatives to "That's so gay," such as, "I don't like that." Make the list into a poster and display it on the wall of your classroom to remind everyone.

STEP 3

Invite a local LGBTQ+ group or youth group to come and give an assembly at your school. Meeting the LGBTQ+ community will help people who use homophobic language to see that they are insulting others and will hopefully inspire them to change.

STEP 4

Host a book club and read books with LGBTQ+ characters. Try to choose books written by LGBTQ+ authors, as they have the best insight into what it is like to be LGBTQ+. Afterward, discuss your thoughts on the book with your friends. What did you learn?

BODIES

Our bodies come in all shapes and sizes. However, this isn't always reflected in our society. Physically disabled people can find it hard to move around because of a lack of accessibility. There is also prejudice against people with larger bodies.

GETTING AROUND

The needs of people with physical disabilities are not always considered when public spaces are planned. They are fitted with steps, rather than ramps. Public transport vehicles often don't have enough space for multiple wheelchairs. These issues make it very hard for people with physical disabilities to move around, which restricts their right to freedom and independence.

THINK ABOUT IT

To give disabled people the same right to freedom as non-disabled people, existing buildings need to be adapted and new spaces built with disabled access. How accessible is your school? Talk to your teachers about making it more disability-friendly.

DISABILITY DISCRIMINATION

People with disabilities also face prejudice in education and at work. They often don't receive the support that they need at school, which means that they can't fulfill their potential. Employers often incorrectly believe that disabled people are less capable and productive than non-disabled people, so they are less likely to hire them. Disabled people are also paid much less for the work that they do.

In the U.S., disabled people are twice as likely to be unemployed as non-disabled people.

SHAPES AND SIZES

Prejudice against overweight or obese people is extremely common. Unlike other forms of prejudice, which are considered unacceptable in most parts of society, prejudice against overweight people is normalized. It's common to see fat jokes in TV shows or films. Many larger people are criticized, bullied, and told to lose weight. This is unacceptable, as everyone has the right to feel happy in their own body.

Because prejudice against larger bodies is so widespread, we are surrounded by images of bodies that don't look like average ones. These images try to convince us that thin bodies are better than larger bodies, and therefore thin people are superior to bigger people.

The most important thing is to have a healthy body, and healthy bodies come in many sizes. Try these tips to boost your body image and get body positive.

STEP 1

Surround yourself with a diverse range of different bodies. TV, films, and magazines often only show thin bodies that have been digitally altered to look skinnier. This has a negative impact on people's body image and mental health. See if you can find media coverage that shows people of a range of sizes instead.

STEP 2

Focus on what your body can do, not what it looks like. Is your body strong or flexible or fast? Think about your strengths and celebrate them!

STEP 3

Keep your body in good health so that you can feel your best. Eat a balanced diet to fuel your body, made up of carbohydrates, protein, healthy fats, and lots of fruits and vegetables. Junk food is fine once in a while, but it can make you unwell if you eat it every day.

STEP 4

Do exercise to keep your body strong and healthy. It might be a team sport, such as basketball, or something you do on your own, such as swimming or speed walking. Try out different options until you find something you enjoy.

 How do you feel when someone criticizes what you eat? It might be because it's unhealthy or because it is healthy. Don't comment on what other people eat, other than to say how delicious it looks! It only makes people feel bad.

STEP 5

Instead of complimenting people on their bodies, focus on other things that are far more important, such as their personality. The size and shape of your body has no connection to how good you are as a person. Congratulate your friends for their achievements, rather than their bodies.

AGE

Prejudice because of age, or ageism, is something that most people will experience at some point in their life. Both young and older people can feel patronized, or treated as if others don't take them seriously. In addition to this, older people often experience serious discrimination because of their age.

AT WORK

Ageism against older people can often be seen in the workplace. People's prejudices lead them to believe that older people are slow or don't understand modern technology. As a result, they are less likely to hire them and so it can be hard for older people to find jobs.

ELDERLY CARE

Older people can also find it hard to get good healthcare. It can be seen as less of a priority to treat older people, as they won't live as long as younger people. Some older people can themselves be ageist. They underestimate what they are capable of doing and assume they can't do certain things because they are "too old."

Adults with positive attitudes about older people can live up to 7.5 years longer than older adults with ageist opinions.

GETTING OLD

Unlike some prejudices, the vast majority of us will experience what it is like to be old. Fighting ageism will help the current elderly population to be treated with more respect and make things better for our future selves. It is particularly important to address ageism as advances in medicine are helping people to live longer and the elderly population is growing.

LISTENING TO EVERYBODY

People often dismiss young and older people. They consider that young people don't have any experience or knowledge of the world, while older people are thought to have lost touch with the modern world. However, both groups have very important insights. Young people are the next generation that will inherit the planet, so their thoughts count. Older people have life experience and it's important to listen to them to avoid making the same mistakes.

BE THE CHANGE, SPREAD THE WORD

>> **The more people who stand up against prejudice and discrimination, the greater the impact will be. Here are some ways to campaign for change and persuade others to do the same.**

PARTY TIME

Host a party at school and invite the people in your class to bring in dishes that they enjoy eating at home. This will help everyone to learn more about the diverse traditions and backgrounds of their classmates. Check about food allergies first and ask an adult to help you prepare the food.

CELEBRATE PRIDE

Many towns and cities have a Pride day, week, or even month, when members of the LGBTQ+ community and allies come together to celebrate as a community, raise awareness, and fight against prejudice and discrimination. There are often Pride parades and other special events, such as talks, film showings, and plays. Find out if there is a Pride celebration or event near you and attend with an adult.

HOST A SCREENING

Host a film screening at home or at school, showing a film that deals with the themes of prejudice and discrimination. It could be a documentary, such as *He Named Me Malala*, about Malala Yousafzai, the young Pakistani activist who fights for girls' rights to an education. Or it could be a fictional film, such as *Billy Elliot*, which is about a boy ballet dancer. Discuss your thoughts on the film afterwards.

WRITE TO YOUR LOCAL POLITICIAN

Find out who your local government officials are and write to them about any problems with prejudice or discrimination in your area. For example, there may be issues with accessible transportation routes for disabled people. The more people that contact an official the better, so ask your friends and family to join you or start a petition.

THINK AND ACT

Can you come up with some other creative ways to **combat prejudice and discrimination?**

Glossary

ageism – prejudice or discrimination against someone because of their age

agnostic – someone who does not know if God exists

ally – someone who supports a group, even if they don't belong to it

atheist – someone who does not believe in God or any gods

cisgender – someone born with the gender that they identify with

cultural appropriation – when someone takes elements of a different culture or group to which they don't belong, without acknowledging where they come from

discrimination – unfair treatment of someone because they are part of a certain group

diverse – including many types of people or things

fake news – false information disguised as true information, which is designed to trick people

fundamentalist – someone who believes in an extreme form of a religion

gender – being male, female, or another gender identity

gender identity – a person's feeling of which gender they are

hate crime – a crime committed against someone because they belong (or appear to belong) to a certain group

homophobia – prejudice or discrimination against someone because they are gay

human right – a basic thing that everyone should have or be able to do, just because they are human

Islam – the Muslim religion

media – TV, film, magazines, internet, and newspapers

Muslim – someone who belongs to the religion of Islam and worships Allah

peer pressure – the influence of a group to make everyone in the group behave in the same way

privilege – advantages that someone has because of a group that they belong to

race – a group of people with similar physical characteristics

racism – prejudice or discrimination against someone because of their race

sexism – prejudice or discrimination against someone because of their gender

sexual orientation – the type of people a person is attracted to, such as the same gender or the opposite gender

stereotype – a set idea that people have about what someone or something is like

terrorism – using fear or violence to scare people to try to make them think a certain way

transgender – someone who feels that they are not the same gender as the one they were said to have at birth